BEST OF THE DRY YEARS

BEST OF THE DRY YEARS

2012—2016

JOHN DOFFLEMYER

Versions of these poems have previously appeared in *Dry Crik Journal—Perspectives from the Ranch*, a weblog, and some from the previously published chapbooks "Gate Left Open", "Wind Under My Skin" and "Homemaking" from Dry Crik Press.

Front cover photo: John Dofflemyer
Back cover photo: Robbin Dofflemyer

ISBN: 1883081084
ISBN: 13: 9781883081089

Dry Crik Press
P.O. Box 44320
Lemon Cove, CA 93244

for Robbin, with love

FORWARD

Nearly everyone in California has been tested by the past four years of drought, the driest in recorded history, perhaps in a millennium by some accounts. Like most of our neighbors, we've been forced to sell half of our cows due to a lack of feed and stockwater. We were finally blessed with a wet spring in 2016, leaving us ample dry grass through the summer and fall. Selectively culled, the genetics of our reduced cowherd have actually benefited from the drought. But even as I write now at the first of December, with a good start to our grass season, predictions from the weather gurus remain dry.

We have grown older and a little tougher, while being humbled to new extremes. We will wear these scars like the ranch wears skeletons of nearly half of its oak tree population, but we will be resilient and again productive. During these dry years, it has taken the two of us, fully invested in the ranch, to gain a renewed appreciation for one another, for the land, and for a refined spirituality that we will always carry forward. While finding new depths to our vulnerabilities, season after season of dust and dry times, we've also found a new assurance in one another and a trust in Nature as we adapt. This is our poetic journal grounded in this landscape, a tiny wrinkle in the southern Sierra Nevada foothills.

POEMS

GRAVITY

I am growing downward,
smaller, one among the grasses.
- Wendell Berry ("Thirty More Years")

GRAVITY

I knew when I was young
and proud, I had found my place
on this ground—my limbs

could support me for as long
as they were sound—living
where the work was hard.

I was not afraid of time
and grinned at gravity,
rode the edges of ridges down

behind cattle, shaping me
to fit this landscape
eventually.

I scratch among the grasses now,
learn the language of birds
and flowers, the expression

of horses and families of cattle—
all the tattered glories of youth
bent closer to what counts.

MY FATHER FARMING

We had water enough for play in furrows
with scraps of wood, leaves for sails,
regattas on rivers pumped from underground.

All the magic that children take for granted
swirled to the hum of electricity, twenty-horse
pumps like Buddhas squat in orchard rows

my father farmed for wagonloads of fruit
ripe for the rail, packed by women's hands
for the road on diesel trucks to distant places.

His silhouette crosses deep within vineyard rows,
early morning, late afternoon, hoe in hand—
his pirate's cutlass, swashbuckling open-topped

overshoes—checking water, irrigating grapes
at seventy, or so I think at sixty-eight, knowing
now what drew him to the earth he flourished.

THE GROUND

We know the ground
as well as we want,
its traps a horseback

o'er its rocky face
we flew with flapping
wings of youth

we gave names to—
plus to the peaceful
we are drawn to

where the cattle
always feel
like gathering.

Seasons of instruction
in the senses, it knows
what the future does not.

WHEN WE WERE BOYS

I read outrage from old hinterland poets
on Facebook to stir my blood, enflame
my brain, pretend that words might quell

injustice with compassion, find humanity
commonplace, or search old dialogues:
mountains, rivers and streams, for peace—

translations to bring home from foreign
lands and times that seem to work here
for a little while. I read to write

when I'm tongue-tied, lend my gravelly
voice to the ancient chorus and try
to sound nice, only to find assonance

puts most folks to sleep. No one needs
to read anymore, translate marks on paper
into better thoughts than when we started—

now that we have open minds and let
technology have its way with us, do it
all as we lay back to enjoy the ride.

No one needs to saddle-up in the dark,
untrack cold-backed broncs to mount
before going to work—they all had names

and personalities when we were boys.
No one needs to reach inside for more
than what we thought we had in those days.

TUITION

Education was cheaper in the old days
when we memorized dates, declined verbs
and parsed sentences to pieces—

fell in and out of love like puppies
chasing the next pair of shoes
to try on, or not—that's how we learned

about ourselves. All my teachers are gone,
or busy getting old, but their younger selves
reside in my brain, fuzzy faces reminding me

that honesty is terribly hard to come by.
Everything we need to know is almost free:
an easy payment plan as long as I remember.

THE WORK

I realize that in terms of body and spirit,
body grows sick while spirit's immune,
- Po Chü-i ("Climbing Mountains in Dream")

Like a wall, hooks in hand,
I've scaled bales of hay stacked
too far off the ground to fall

for nearly fifty winters, boot toes
feeling for a crack and hang
while synapse talks to flesh—

a longer conversation now
for this ascent. I can fly
in my dreams, scramble

like a squirrel up a tree.
Awake: my spirit intact, in touch
with heart and mind's belief

in these old knees they will escape
after the truck is loaded, cattle
fed—when the work is done.

SMALL TOWNS

There is no hiding within
rural communities, the gossip hubs
of small towns team with news

at the doughnut shop, the feed store
trading in common tragedies:
DUIs, divorces, suicides.

We learn to live with guilt, grab
hold to stand beside the twisted
truth of being human, wear

the shame of each unpolished flaw
to endure self-inflicted tortures
until we shed this flesh.

No one is anonymous, no passing
face on the street. But sometimes
all the imperfections bloom

beyond the anguish, each petal
turned skyward to drink up the sun
and rain—and we are whole

for moments that no one has words
to describe, or time to take
to indulge in such nonsense.

THE MOUNTAINS

At their feet, I must leave home—
the house, the canyon, to see them.
At the overpass between Exeter

and Visalia, when at cloudy dawn
they became my mother's rumpled
bedclothes as she courted death,

the Sierras cloaked in a gossamer mist
that embraced me. Or just south
of Lemon Cove, up the Kaweah's long,

open throat, sharp-toothed peaks
of granite scree reach into the sky,
changing moods in every light.

A man must have mountains
to lose the nonsense to get to—
a distant and steep ascent

for the spirit, soul and flesh—
a place safe to wander fire to fire,
star to star, to drink from snowmelt.

Wide arms open, they welcome me
as I come home from town
to lay down at their wrinkled feet.

THE TROUBLE WITH HEROES

After the war,
hats and horses,
black and white heroics
helped us forget
Hitler and Hiroshima,
helped heal and shape
half of humanity hooked
on Hollywood cowboys.

I lived close to the stars,
slept near the fire,
drank from a stream
of tomorrows
that have arrived
twenty thousand times
working towards
this moment in a poem:

glimpses of reckless youth
and luck at the Longbranch
replaced by another tribe
of younger men
wild, woolly and tough.
With each wind-whipped rumor,
I worry more about them
than I did myself.

SIESTA

My black and white
horseback heroes
still shoot it out,

subdue evil,
herk and jerk to leave
the hitching rack—

the Westerns Channel
as I lay down
to take a nap,

now knowing how
each episode
always ends—

familiar voices
comfort me
to believe the West

is wild and safe
from all the mean
and greedy men

we've since seen,
a lullaby guaranteed
for sleep.

WAY OUT WEST, 2016

We know the feeling of corrals
in airports, and prepare ourselves
to be bunched-up, to wait in lines
at every gate—to follow rules
for humans. We should have seen
the red fire trucks as an omen,
but we loaded-up, anyway,
found our seats and waited.

I was a mountain man in another life
dodging Indians and ole Ephraim,
knew them all and their stories
and started reading. About the time
Hugh Glass met the grizzly's cubs,
the captain was on the intercom
to say it'll be short, or a long wait
to leave for Dallas, to find the trouble
with the engine gauge, *maybe just
a loose wire.* I am a slow reader,
but by the time they started patching
Hugh Glass's bloody body up,

we deplaned to rebook our flight—
190 head, three hours in the lead-up
to be processed. No way to get
to Dallas and keep the four of us
together, no other plane to haul

the human cargo—no way to share
awards and ceremony. (*They kill
the man*, anyway, Jeffers said).

Out West beyond the claustrophobe,
we should be proud of plans
that we expect—that have to get
the work done, where we depend
on few. But in these corrals, numb
humans herding humans used to
corporate calculations failing—
we treat ourselves and cattle better.

APART

Before and after the weather report
we get news from far away places:
tragedies and terrible things

that want to linger in our minds
asking questions—but we don't like
the answers that must be true

about the nature of humans opposed
to peace, that are driven to leave
horrible impressions behind.

We watch the cows come into water
in a well-spaced line, taking turns
at the trough, then count quail babies

herded on the lawn to escape the cats.
Within a crease among so many others
on the durable hide of this planet,

we inhabit a canyon shaped
by the allocation of water
apart from the world outside.

JULY 1, 2016

Outside in the shade, the two-speed fan
is like an oscillating blow torch
offering velocity to 110 degrees—

yellow pad and pencil, my red wine
warm as a tepid cup of tea,
I listen to Outlaw on Sirius wondering

if any of us can make a difference
to how the world shakes-out after
another summer of half-baked promises,

malevolent campaigns cooking-up
new recipes to wear upon
the ageless face of God.

Dawn cool through the screen door,
gold leaf print upon a purple coffee cup:
MT. SENTINEL RANCH, 1898 – 1998.

for Francis Gardner
1942 -2016

DURABLE

We meet at the end of generations
    of pioneers here
    after 160 years,
    all related since
    that first local election
    cast by 27 men—
    the tie broken
    by a trapper
    from Dry Creek
    wined and dined
    at Nate Vise's fort
    a week before the vote.

Mom and pop cow outfits and farmers,
we tend and claim our space—
    our own language
    and hands-on humor
    handed down
    by surviving
    miscalculations.
    More and more
    we lean on
    the old sayings
    we were raised
    to recite.

Most of what we know
    we learned
    the hard way
    about ourselves—
    but most of all
    we've learned to laugh
    at change at last.

WEED SEED

...my life
a patient willing descent into the grass.
- Wendell Berry ("The Wish To Be Generous")

Hemmed in silver moonlight, scattered
clouds linger over hills, no wet reflection
of the porch light. She has come and gone

without waking me with thunder, pellets
on the roof, not a leaky drip from the eave,
leaving nothing to remember her passing

by—not even her musty petrichor perfume
in the damp dark air to soothe my senses—
gone without a thought of waking me.

From a distance in the daylight, islands
of purple filaree look like dirt in graying
green, rolling dusty plumes follow cows

into water, yet they don't seem to worry
into another winter without rain. Too
familiar, I read the signs with each synapse

shortened by the hard and dry. Too long
in the same place, I can see the weather
and the world have changed around me—

changed me as I retreat and try to adapt
like summer weed seeds over time:
impervious to thirst and political herbicides.

MANIFEST DESTINY

It was swamp between the rivers and creeks
of melted snow, men claiming ground by boat,
a century of floods and drought before the dam

slowed the river down to fit furrows and ditches
to feed the world, the course of water left in crops
we farmed with mules before the teams of tractors

grew so big and smart as not to need a man
to guide them. We made towns look like cities
with cool conditioned air, still digging deeper

for pockets of water where no river flows.
Someday, she will take her ground back
from the idols and graven images of rock star

convenience. Someday we may balance joy
with work instead of wages, find eyes to see
the obvious is less than what we think we need.

WEATHER CHANGE

I turn away, blinded by November's
first light, Redbud hearts enflamed
with last season's feed on green

burning yellows between dark shadows
with the election, with disbelief.
I retreat to calm counsel with cattle:

scattered pairs, calves fresh with life
finding legs to fly—buck and run
figure-eights without direction always

circling back, showing off for mom.
We will work the heifers anyway—
give them everything we can

to make them attractive to Wagyu,
their first bulls. And we will wait,
as we always do, for rainy days.

TOO OLD TO VOTE

O wonder!
How many goodly creature are there here!
How beauteous mankind is!
O brave new world, That has such people in't.
- William Shakespeare ("The Tempest")

I am too old to vote
for the least offensive—
too old to believe
raucous rhetoric,
philosophies that fan
the flames of fear
to obtain heaven
early on this earth.

I have seen enough
bigotry and greed
squirming beneath the raiment
of righteousness—
that need evil foes to exist,
when war is peace.

All the good in this world
is not for sale, cannot be carved
from the heart of humanity,
or extinguished by authority—
it casts no vote but to survive
our nasty campaigns and elections.

STAGE MANAGER

After awhile in a place, the trees we plant,
fertilize and irrigate for summer shade
and privacy need to be pruned to see

the pasture between us and the road,
as cows and calves become autumn's
evening entertainment waiting

for a rain beneath a waxing moon
and the ridgeline's jagged shadow
cast across a canyon greening—

    the phone rings inside
    lamenting the election
    and everything it means:

no more robot recordings begging money
and votes, four times a day, for candidates
and propositions I know nothing about.

Yet sure of another set of rules and taxes
to pay for agencies and enforcement
to make the majority feel better

about this crazy world. I need to raise
the curtain, cut another limb to sooner
see who or what's coming up the road.

BASIC STUFF

Writing poetry in the dark
before moving cows
and fresh calves
to better pasture,
I ask about the weather
on TV I've missed
over a weekend of
making more from less water
while you've planted seeds
for a fall garden—more
hopeful than ever before.

You say, 'More of the same
for the next few days, cooler.'
Two years of dust and drought
have worn us down to basic stuff—
and we like what we see
in one another.

THE BIRD AND ANIMAL PEOPLE

When the old-time bird and animal people created Mi'eh, the Indians, they took new forms and went away to the mountains to live as we see them today.
- F. F. Latta ("California Indian Folklore")

RAIN SONGS

and holy
days asleep in the calendar wake up and chime.
- William Stafford ("How You Know")

Tree frogs awake in the dark,
in the rain, a steady wave of chorusing
croaks upon croak—thousands

clear the air in their throats
again and again, prolong moments
no one else seems to want.

I pause in my tracks listening
deep into the wet blackness to a holy
tradition begun before man.

GOLDEN EAGLE

Cultivating a native life,
we pause for totems,
let them tell us
what they think—
who they are.

Some count on us
to stir the grass
and follow, and some
to listen when we drink
coffee or wine outside.

Claiming the roost
of loving crow mates,
a Golden Eagle lights
for a closer look at us—
and we are blessed.

Finding his feather
left ahead, we believe
in something
more common
than wild,

of talismans
from moments
we never forget—
hoping to leave
as much.

ODE TO THE BULLFROG

It's not a clean world
where frogs can live like kings
on their own island

apart from the main
stream, where stagnant
boils under the summer sun

with new life they trust
will keep them fed
tomorrow. So far

from our marsh
and mire beginnings,
we tidy up instead.

RAINBOW TROUT

If you are a fish,
you find an eddy
behind a boulder

or a cutbank
shadowed
by a tree root

where Snallygasters
ride the current
snowmelt.

We swim upstream
for the perfect place
to make our livings—

where rivers start
close to the stars,
deep in the pines,

where water falls
fast and cold
all year long—

but always swimming
against the flow
just to hold our own.

HUNTER

Not too old to hunt,
it is my eyes that crave
the grace of wild things,

that tell the boy inside
to take another look,
focus while he can.

I have tracked, squeezed
the trigger, gutted, skinned
and hung the flesh

over flames, told the stories
within these mountains
where I became a man

who hunts for pleasure,
for sign each day—
for what he's never seen.

for Matt St. Martin

MONUMENTS

The storms line up
like diesel trucks
in the slow lane,

hills green
and scattered cattle
graze ridgetops.

I had forgotten how
heaven looked,
learning to live

with dust and smoke,
all shades of brown—
years without water.

We cannot reduce
all the ghoulish skeletons
to cordwood, clear

these monuments of oak
from mind or eye.
They will remind us

of who we came to be
to survive
what they could not.

WOE BE TO INTRUDERS

Clinging to a willow branch
above the cattails, singing
across the pond at dawn,

this world is small enough
for herons and mud hens,
a loan goose and bullfrogs—

all the drama necessary
for a rich full life
of trying to get along.

ROADRUNNERS AT DAWN

In the early stillness
when sky is white
above the ridgeline,

hollow coos
of Roadrunners
spill off hillsides,

sounds sprinkling
almost like a song
for themselves—

or for all of us
who have endured
years of drought

to rise early
to carry on
upon dry dirt.

Blessed are birds—
may their gods
become ours.

KILLDEER

I could have been born a bird
on a gravel island in the creek,
learn to hide in a small world

before I found the gentle grace
to fly, hop rock to rock
as mother drew intruders off

with shoreline flaps of her white
petticoats, feigning injury,
crying seriously in low circles.

I could have been born a bird
without certainty, without worries
about my death or politics.

RATTLESNAKES

In a world tall with grasses,
wild oats and rosy thatches
of dry filaree, we seldom see

our feet upon the earth.
In frequented places
like water troughs and barns,

like vegetable gardens
saving trips to town,
we are prejudiced—

react without a thought
against a race of snakes
that want no trouble,

to claim the space
in which we travel
with a shovel.

for Terri

SIGN OF SOMETHING

The pair of bald eagles
returning early to ride
our foothill thermals

elicits surprise, 'what
do they know that we don't,'
we agree to say.

No water, no place
to fish in a four year drought—
a sign of something.

DREAMS IN DROUGHT

Good bug year:
Daddy Longlegs
on a wet paint wall,
Crane Fly waiting
for me to dry
and hang my towel
back, herds of Earwigs
hiding between the leaves
of artichokes, and bitter
gnats drowning
in my uncovered wine.
Most don't bite

but feed the Phoebes
and one another
in the springtime,
summer, fall.
Hatch upon hatch,
I think of casting
to eddies, riding riffles,
the splash and set
of hook, playing
and landing trout
if there were
any rivers running.

DOES-IN-WAITING

Hide-outs saved for sane
discussions, always listening
between short sentences

for advances within the dry
and brittle skeletons of spring—
we could forever be nervous

deer on the rebound, come back
to ricochet within a shrinking
wild that we have helped consume.

On the outskirts, perhaps
we feel it now approaching, wind
the scent of human arrogance

surrounding us, that we succumb to
out of necessity knowing
we're headed in the wrong direction.

OBITUARY

Bright color in the thin shade
of dry casualties: proud skeletons
of fathers and grandfathers,

generations of Blue Oaks standing
stoically against the sky, against
time as the earth comes alive.

Each silent prayer is a short nod
in passing—too many decomposing
monuments for long eulogies

no one will remember—
we dance past death
as the last obstacle to life.

GRASS

While we slept, the grass grew
an inch overnight beneath the clouds
and passing showers, working overtime,

as the dry earth spun beneath them—
as the creek edged down through sand
and gravel, seeping over the granite dikes

that lump its bed, towards the river
and settlements downstream. I dreamed
we were the end of the line

living on a lake amid thick timber,
fat fish flashing bellies to the sun
and fresh meat hung in a tree.

No other world beyond but more
of the same, working on its own—
no children slain in schools for effect,

no political charades, no slaves
to bankers banking on superfluous debt—
and the grass grew taller, while we slept.

SPRING CROWS

They shiver after
making love on a dead branch
facing the future.

TURKEY VULTURE

Busy with cleanup,
little time to say hello
or come much closer.

THREE GEESE

Off the road, three geese
feel safe, wait for barley hay—
one without a mate.

BUZZARDS

Gathering deacons
waiting between casualties
dream of misfortune.

SUMMER

July dragonflies
near collisions of color
even in dry times.

POLLEN

Busy as a bee
with the basics, it's normal
to get some on you.

LIKE BUMBLEBEES

We jump into spring
without looking or thinking,
craving wild nectar.

ANOTHER SURVIVOR

Gun in the scabbard
shooting with a camera
the world stays the same.

BLACKTAIL BUCKS

Blurs that stir the heart
banked in brush without a shot
for another day.

112 DEGREE DAZE

Low hills worn smooth as flesh,
summer blonds with different shades
of grazing play in one another's shadow

at dusk and dawn, a plain and treeless
nakedness I trace, pausing with my eyes,
to touch ridges, gaps and valleys falling

into Live Oak canyons, gentle slopes frozen
in an undulating moment drawn and prolonged
with each breath in uncertain light—slipping

slightly, she comes alive, dressing differently
with each season. At work early, young herons
greet me. We nod and say good morning.

NOWHERE
PEOPLE

You ask why I've settled in these emerald mountains:
I smile, mind of itself perfectly idle, and say nothing.

Peach blossoms drift streamwater away deep in mystery
here, another heaven and earth, nowhere people know.
- Wang Wei ("Mountain Dialogue")

NOWHERE PEOPLE

To and from their peach tree roost
the quail trail in at dawn and dusk
like heavy heifers on parade

from shade to water trough
before they graze the waves of dry,
blond hillsides bent to a breeze.

An evening tree frog leaves a centerpiece
of succulents at six o'clock, short hops
to table's edge and leaps for misters

on timers, scales the green swords of iris
for the wet scent of lavender and more—
crawls back at dawn like a drunk home.

We meet the mystery of nowhere
in a slow dance of seasonal cycles
returning new over and over again.

NEIGHBORS

We wish success for all our neighbors, fat
calves and money enough to buy good bulls
looking for work on our side of the fence,
and ours on theirs, despite best intentions.

Today, old neighbors come to brand calves
with respect—rope, stretch and vaccinate
rambunctious children to a slow waltz—
to share the bounty of our heritage

despite the drought, despite the cows
we had to sell to save the others and ourselves.
Character from this ground, we have survived
the weather and the marketplace.

THE DANCE

In the branding pen
the steady dance of old hands
celebrating spring.

BRAND OF LIFE

We ride for a brand
of life in open spaces
while the iron is hot.

GATHERING TO BRAND

Neighbors visiting
behind young girls and babies
headed to the gate.

FINDING ORDINARY

Old men in the branding pen
hope for grace

to find the feel of a singing loop
slide between their fingers—

of hoof dance timed and shaped
to catch two feet, slack to dally horn

come tight, as if it were nothing
out of the ordinary.

LA DIFFÉRENCE

Horseback, the girls work
cattle in the dust, sort cows
from calves before hauling

off the hill to the weaning pen:
a quiet dance to a rhythm
I can only see through boards

as cows ask with their eyes
before moving towards the open
space a horse has made

to leave their calves behind.
No loud bravado spurring
pirouettes into dirt clouds.

I turn away and walk
to the pickups and goosenecks—
remove my maleness

from these corrals that hold
a hundred years of urgent
echoes: men making mistakes

to invent new profanities.
Instead, the perfect sense
of girls instructing girls.

YOU SHOULD KNOW

You should know how
to read sign, find water,
follow tracks and stars
and tell about it—how
to start a fire in the rain
skin a rabbit, cook the meat
and pick your teeth with a bone.

You should know how
to make the mundane rich
with detail and symbolism,
start your own religion, quietly—
to look through the eyes
of animals, trees and birds
to see yourself as common.

You should know how
to draw lines, share space
and learn to help.
You should know how
to create the kind of joy
you cannot buy
with cash or credit.

IN PLACE

I have forgotten
lots of things,
left them on the job,

or like tools
in the weeds
by mistake.

If any good
comes from drought,
it's finding things

and remembering
how and who
we've been

without one another—
sweet reunion with
my pipe wrench friend.

LIVING COLOR

My feet have slowed—
my eye measures distance
and my mind weighs

the importance of moving
as I withdraw
from all the magic

flashing the horizon
like explosions
of another war

that will not wound me,
fatally. This time
is mine to spend,

frugally. Summer sighs
into September shadows
as I wait for storms

to wash the outside
world clean away.
Too old to play football

or politics anymore,
I hear colors sing
without a score.

IN SEPTEMBER

Progress parallels the creek,
follows a crumbling dirt track paved
up canyon past the end of power poles

and the double yellow line,
the busy bulk of it beyond
the hazy ridgeline—

beyond thinking past water
when the creek is dry
in September.

Caravans of Christians
craving altitude, the new shine
of fifth-wheels pulling for the pines—

the guttural rumble, leather herds
of Harleys and the bright spandex
of cyclists pass us by

as if we were a landscape
to endure along the way
to something better.

PERSPECTIVE

There is no blank sheet—
no white, unblemished page
on which to letter words
together, even in the highlands.

Once when I was there in awe
and almost nothing, irrelevant
but to breathe and drink from streams
of melting snow off peaks

like granite teeth sunk into the blue,
blue sky, lost in my insignificance—
the paper I carried from the world
below was smudged and dirty.

So it is with humans, never free,
never clean enough to pen words
without shadows, without darkness
leaking in between the haze of stars.

NO URGENCY

But traces in quiet fog:
ridgeline of the barn roof,
cold parts of the corral

float in and out of gray
closing in upon our fire—
forms of horses look

for hazy movement
in this fuzzy moment
shut away from hills

and towns beyond, the world
and its miseries. All
we have accomplished near

at hand, close to fading
into nothingness
and I am relieved

of the weight of urgency—
perfectly helpless
to change a thing.

DISCLAIMER

> *That I*
> *may have spoken well*
> *at times, is not natural.*
> *A wonder is what it is.*
> - Wendell Berry ("A Warning To My Readers")

Those who work beside me hear
the gerunds and gerundives mesh
with coarser nouns and verbs
that flourish on unlevel landscapes
among the animals and birds,

or whispered under breath
in politer conversation
like adding grain to polished wood—
profane accents and accidents
straining to leap from my tongue.

UNTAMED SILENCE

Heading into winter, black cows yet fat
sucking calves—damp, thick-piled green after rain—
everyone is clean and shiny off the hill, parading
to water early to laze in the shade. Pages

of poetry shuffle across a desk messy with business,
an untitled collection scattered and spread,
collected and clipped faraway in my head
from our family of cows, from short remarks:

our song of words and phrases overflowing
with the water troughs at Windmill Spring,
spilling too spontaneously to require editing.
We needed to collaborate, to escape the loud

and demanding devils too close to home.
In this place, we are blessed with native eyes
and forgotten tongues—where we can relate
long poems in the luxury of untamed silence.

LEAVING WITH STAFFORD

I imagine that the young men
I went to school with have retired
by now, given up their desks
for free-wheeling possibilities

to coast downhill grades, collecting
their rewards and all the promises made
to themselves, over and over again.
I truly wish them all the best.

And I suspect the girls have become
wise grandmothers with practical advice,
keeping secrets in ceramic cookie jars
with noisy lids like I remember.

Leaving with Stafford, I retire
from a world too large to digest,
and go to that far place for the familiar
sign, those recognizable tracks

where wild makes sense of circumstance.
We are collecting short stories
like mushrooms in wicker baskets
before they fade and melt into the ground,

discussing how we'll sauté them over fire
in butter and garlic to melt in our mouths
instead. Already we can feel their wild
flavor rage in our veins, like venison,

as we peel old flesh, find keen eyes.
All the ghosts will rise beneath the stars
to gather at our fire, faces flickering
in the darkness to share the light.

LOGGING TRUCKS

Dead cedars, yellow pine
roll off the mountain
on trucks, great rounds felled

after drought
down a narrow road
to be ground

into toothpicks, I'm told.
Under the leaky flume
on the Middle Fork,

a Kenworth edged
the '57 Ford wagon full
of kids and groceries

to a stop, red bark
dripping, hanging like hair—
we held our breath.

Breaking black silence,
a diesel rumbles upcanyon
at four, piggyback, phallic

trailer tongue angled up,
pointing to Eshom
as headlights pass,

to remove the dead
witnesses
to Ghost Dances past.

DREAMS

A slice of time incised from ranch
routines, an Indian poet-in-residence
for a week, Kerouac on the wing

escaping Montana's sub-zero to write
about dreams. He thinks in Crow,
undulating hands stroke the grace

between them, never touching speak,
pleasant sounds of rushing water gush
from his lips I almost understand.

I envy this bear of a man
who brings brightly painted ponies
and the Little Big Horn with him,

the feathered glory of reenactments
and contact with the old chiefs
breathing past and present here

upon my skin. What a way to go out,
to become one with time, turn the soul
loose and gather 'round the fire

of mountain men, all the old cowboys
and pioneers, all the natives done with
trying to make a living on this ground.

for Henry Real Bird

LISTENING IN FOG

And, nothing himself, behold
Nothing that is not there and the nothing that is.
- Wallace Stevens ("The Snow Man")

Always the backdrop
of deep pipe songs
awakening at dawn—
Roadrunners in rockpiles
like coyotes at night
finding one another.
Or the late November chill
of sequestered bulls
pacing the barbed wire,
their primal trumpeting
echoes up and down canyon
searching for the company
of work, sweet work.
The quiet moments
in between are cold
before and after
a good hard rain
when fog rolls in,
up canyon,
spilling over ridges
to wall the world away
in opaque gray

swallowing sound
to leave you lost,
disconnected, alone
with only the thought
of becoming nothing.

CHANCE

Dry hills soft, come dusk
before a promised chance
of rain, blond fuzz

of empty-headed grasses
teased by gusts
beg to embrace me,

to become lost
in the folds of canyons
and draws, absorbed

as someday I will be.
Dark breezes stir the senses
with anticipation,

transform baked clay
to breathing slopes
of warm flesh

and I am comforted—
home at last,
a chance for peace.

FROM THIS EARTH

To leave this world in spring,
they have gone on
to grace another space—

hob-nob with the gods
as we remain remembering
to the soothing sound of rain

dark upon our roofs.
Cut-off low out of the south
will linger into a gray

daybreak, and I will absorb
their passing with welcome nods
of understanding

when I turn myself loose
to gaze and search for sign
upon this landscape.

Song and laughter
from this earth,
Vaya con Dios!

> *for Pat Richardson*
> *and Merle Haggard*

CEREMONY

Blue Oak rounds too big for the woodstove
collect near the splitter in a pile—energy
stored in rings of sun, years of rain—
the severed dead, hard and dry inside.

We look ahead to ceremony, prepare
as we go, set aside the burls and forks,
too twisted to split, for the outside fire
and generations of flickering faces.

I see my mother in my grand-daughter's
eyes, leave us for a moment for the flames
lapping the remains of a stump—the call
from beyond that burns within us all—

she is drawn away. It is the coming back
to her mother's lap, her bemused recognition
of going somewhere within white coals
beyond this half-circle of family

that I see my mother in her face
while the meat cooks. We talk, lift glasses
in the smoke that swirls undecidedly
around us, just out of reach of the flames.

Early tracks upon the morning frost,
someone will rise to stir the embers,
to rekindle conversation from cold night
hoping to keep the celebration alive.

DECOMPOSITION

I'm below the snowline
biodegradable as hell.
- Red Shuttleworth ("Café With Slot Machines")

When the taxman finds us,
there's always the argument
over appraisal of this and that

accomplishment, certain failures turned
skyward to face floating white cumulus
with hopes of a more productive afterlife.

The news is too much, poor excuse
for children's stories peddling common sense.
No Aesop, not even the Brothers Grimm

can keep the future in bread crumbs—
no little red hens to do the dirty work,
no hands-on tools for grindstones.

When he comes, we may be out in the barn
with friends, dusty antiques with loose screws
he may overlook if the dogs don't

give us away, so far from the house,
trying to freeze time by supposing
we might have made a difference.

WOOLY CANYON DAWN

Blankets and leather
rest ready for the gather,
cowdogs in the shade.

PAREGIEN RANCH

No day to gather
cattle in a sea of fog—
just wait by the fire.

TARANTULA

An evening walk:
eight hairy legs in concert
with one another.

INGRAINED

I awake with chain saw eyes
measuring fallen trees:

> to die of thirst,
> dividends of drought

thick torsos with loose bark,
little brush to stack

> to clear for grass,
> to cover quail from hawks—

stove wood to haul and split
to hold the cold at bay

> outside the door
> into chimney smoke

and they are beautiful
in death, limbs reaching up

> lengths cut clean
> with sharp eyes

like people to heaven
begging notice, a chance

for purpose yet
and I am looking,

measuring like a tailor
around burls and forks—

old habits stumbling
with weak knees

in and out of dreams
come wintertime.

ANYMORE

Too few days of rain to save for,
                             anymore:
the special jobs on the list of extras
when too wet to get to anywhere
off the road, and you choose jelly
while it pours. The pomegranate tree
I pruned too much bore fruit
with volunteers now big enough
to finish filling gallon jugs with crimson
juice pressed from a jillion seeds
and saved in the freezer, now thawed
waits for sugar and that special
pectin brought to a boil to fill these jars
of translucence sealed to give away
to family and friends for Christmas.
Who saves these things for rainy days?

for Robbin

NOWHERE PEOPLE 2

We are the nowhere people blessed
in nameless places where waves of gold
glint off grasses beyond long shadows

that stream downhill at dawn and dusk,
beyond the instant politic of greed
that lusts for more power over

humanity: all the great hearts secreted
away, shared in private moments as if
outlaws. We are the nowhere people

living an ever-changing dream
of the old ways practiced season
after season, as easily forgotten

as fading chimney smoke—
our ascension from this earth
that flesh cannot escape.

WILDFLOWERS

The wild requires we learn the terrain,
nod to all the plants and animals and birds,
ford the streams and cross the ridges and
tell a good story when we get back home.
- Gary Snyder ("The Etiquette of Freedom")

PRETTY FACES

Over the ridge, friendly families
claim the hillside, pale homesteads
amid a sweep of shadowed green

beg for me to look, first to welcome
me back home, back off the road
two thousand feet below.

Here, now can last a long time—no need
to remember names when everyone
looks the same, ready for a party.

ELEGANT CLARKIA

Not ready long, they reach
for attention, beg to be seen
within the tall dry grass:

pink pulses clinging to the stem
like fairies resting might
if you let yourself believe.

IDES OF MARCH, 2016

A yellow pincushion dances outside
my macro lens, unsteady gusts
I can't follow closely, can't keep up

on my knees. But I know what I want
and hope for something better
than what I see, let the aperture

find bokeh and focus for a fraction
of a second saved for another time
when I need to escape the news—

lose myself, and be this flower
wild and hearty in sandy ground
that grows poor feed for cattle.

Low downcanyon, all shades
of gray after-rain clouds, convoys
of cumulus trailing the storm from west

to east wanting to be thunderheads
as far as I can see of infinity
from the pasture this close up.

- for Jessica

GRAPES IN BLOOM

Muggy morning beneath a raft of clouds
docked against the Sierras steals molecules
of oxygen beside the last hole dug for granddad's

gravel that now traps tailwater from the pasture
in the summer, its dark, stagnant pool teams
with amoeba and paramecium, a fermenting

stench swum only by cormorants and mud hens.
Sweet fragrance on a gust startles my senses
to search the dry grass for color, tree limbs

for blossoms from willow to sycamore,
blackberry to cottonwood, but none in flower
before the forecast Mother's Day thunderstorms.

Perfumed tendrils cling like Christmas lights
from branches and I am drenched in damp
sweet fragrance, taste wild grapes in bloom.

BABY BLUE EYES

Delicate patches
along the creek, they flourish—
mother's favorite.

SIERRA TIDY TIPS

Leaks in a dry spring,
its wild yellow nectar drips
with sweet abundance.

AGOSERIS

Hard to concentrate
under a camera lens
interrupting work.

JIMSON WEED

Flowers beautiful,
but seeds can kill or leave you
talking with the gods.

ORNAMENTS

Christmas in April,
Wild Cucumber pods dry on
dead Manzanita.

WILD HYACINTH

No perfect flower,
yet we hunger for beauty
greater than nature.

BIRD'S EYE GILIA

So many vying
for your attention, easy
to go unnoticed.

BIRD'S EYE GILIA 2

Too many to count,
everyone wants to be
in perfect focus.

KAWEAH BRODIAEA

Hiding in the shadows
and deep in the dry grasses,
no longer extinct.

HOMEMAKING

Perhaps man has a hundred senses,
and when he dies only the five senses
that we know perish with him, and
the other ninety-five remain alive.
- Anton Chekhov ("The Cherry Orchard")

HOMEMAKING

The past walks here, all the dead
horses and livestock men grazing
a hundred and fifty springs—

all the promises and passion spilled
upon this wild mat of grass and flowers,
naked lovers idly pinching petals

along the creek for centuries
within the mottled shade
these same trees have cast, yet see

to keep alive. We have had
our moments here, left ourselves
so wholly that we rise and rest

among them, add our song
to the canyon, our cries to the sky
to forever make our home.

AMONG THE PINES

We live too low, too far down
the mountain to hear
the Canyon Wren sing

for the joy of it, cascade
of octaves, grin in the cedars,
thunder of the river dim.

Our love affair with music
is our own, separate
secrets searching for a song

somewhere on the mountain—
that half-ascension
finding harmony among the pines.

FISH ROCK

Sweet water rises here
from forgotten depths—
Sierra snowmelt streaming
granite cracks under pressure,

underground waterways
clogged with huge trout.
A near escape as the earth
cooled to mark the place.

Words leak out, collect
on paper, fill a trough
open to native myths
locked in rock.

for Sylvia

HIGH SIERRA TALES

We start with trails
that haven't changed
near the top of the world—

    switchbacks stacked
    in scree
    to gaps between
    bare peaks like teeth
    above the timberline
    chewing at the blue,
    blue sky

and the solitude

waiting in ambush
    to welcome you home
    to rainbow trout
    now spawning,
    green backs packed
    in the leak
    of a snowmelt lake
    where white clouds
    float upon water.
    Alone in the smear
    of starlight falling
    upon solid rock,
    granite glows
    like a lantern.

We start with trails
we know to get there.

for Lee and Earl

STATE OF GRAVITY

We are not spirits only
when gravity works
flesh into dirt, pulls
bones into the womb
of all things as roots cling
and search for water.

Like drought-dead oaks
with loosened bark, clumps
of mistletoe hanging black
on the other side of Christmas,
Apollo's hot breath
on our burnt lips kissed

with summer's revenge.
It is not the dark rain
that dissipates strength,
weakens wooden handles:
the hands-on tools
for arms and legs

as hoe and shovel twist
and bow, decompose
beneath unrelenting heat.
We are not spirits yet
to defy mortal forces:
the bodies politique

that wear us down to find
our own serenity within
delirium under the sun.
We will walk with gods
soon enough and envy
this state of gravity.

GOOD MEDICINE

When we gathered this earth,
found its splendid secrets
flourishing, full with flavor,

we believed we had favor
with the gods we acknowledged
everyday—good medicine.

And when we hunted, we learned
to leave our flesh, fill the tracks
before us and read the mind

that left them. It was easy then
to be outside ourselves
to love another, escape together,

go beyond the bounds
of flesh and return
with good medicine.

WONDERMENT

My other voice just beneath the skin,
its echoes muffled by convention
and chained from reason's reach

to speak only to me, quickly and quietly—
my unholy voice of blatant honesty
I can neither temper nor ignore,

telling more than I truly comprehend,
amazes me: a brief non-sequitur
with keen edge, blade like a mirror.

I have grown deaf to crowds chanting
simple mantras as demigods rave—
I keep my counsel with wonderment.

VISITATIONS

I wake to dreams running
with Japhy Rider glowing old,
each awakening begins

a new act, a new setting,
new and easy conversations,
and we are grinning.

I am small in all this,
absorbing each moment
as it unfolds, and fall

into that fuzzy parallel plane
where souls gather,
the dead and alive—

where scientists and governments
cannot touch the caring core
of humanity, where Wall Street

wanes. I wonder now awake
if he remembers me
from last night's sleep.

TAILWATER

The place has changed
where water pooled,
ringed by cattails

at the end
of irrigated pastures
long gone brown

for rock and gravel
royalties that boomed
before the bust.

How many times
have those Mallards
risen in my mind?

My father's words
on a Sabbath saved
from Sunday School,

our ascension
beyond religion
dripping from clouds.

AMONG GODS

The old ways fade
and disappear into the dust—
we leave few tracks

in the mountains,
in the canyons—
our hands are rough.

Red rivers run
through our hearts,
love and logic pulse

our slow composure:
young horseback souls
grown old and weary,

we inhale the pitch
of pines, the cedar
smoke, silhouettes

facing one another
around the fire.
Red cinders rise

to join the stars
of forgotten time
among gods.

for Amy

FOUNDATION

In her nearly ninety years,
Nora Montgomery couldn't remember
hillsides as solid with poppies

as the golden spring of 1978
after two years drought,
cows calving in dust.

Slopes alive, fences leaked
lovers and photographers
from all over—

a glorious reward
for enduring a dry nightmare
early in my career,

the foundation
of a young man's confidence,
a religion he lived by.

AN APRIL FOOL

Life dries up and the dark earth cracks,
crumbles back into its open mouth,
stifling a dusty gasp. Already, I have

forgotten focus, how exactly each detail
hung on the moment, on my half-delirious
plodding one-day-at-a-time for years—

photographs no one wants to share.
But when life rains from the sky,
germinates and steams with spring,

I become an April fool inhaling
as much as I can, storing the miracle
in my veins until I become it,

ultimately. No alabaster walls for me,
no perfect city. Let me laze among
my gods: the water and the weeds.

BEYOND LOCKS

Fence posts and barbed wire:
obstacles for honest people,
may their tribe increase.

NATIVE LADIES

Acorn to oak tree
shade for girls to gossip by
grinding a living.

HOME AFTER RAIN

The cleaning lady
came to sweep the dust away
finally with rain.

THE SOUND OF FURY

It could be explosions at sea
that cloud our sky, dim the peaks
that guide us home at dawn

as thunder cells return to the scene
of the Rough Fire, thermals billowing,
vortex rising in a fire storm.

The mountains wear the violence
that has shaped them, know the sound
of fury in all its beautiful colors.

FEED, WEEDS & WATER

In the dry and dusty years,
we did not ask much
from our night dreams

of brittle details to get by
day by day—no pastoral
pipe dreams, no comedy.

But we indulge the gods
because we must endure
their sense of humor.

THE GOOD SIGNS

Sunday evening, pickup loads of snow
file down the road to town: snowmen
for Visalia, Exeter, Farmersville front yards

to melt and soak into drought-brown lawns
no one's mowed in years—a hurried
passage from mountains to Valley

upon a crumbling blacktop channel—
water that these oaks and sycamores
see only as lumps of white passing at sixty.

The west and south slopes fill-in
with green, purple patches of frost-bitten
filaree that looked like bare dirt, softly

embrace us now as if we were cattle.
Too wet for work that waits outside,
we slowly release winters of urgency

camped at the door and ease into the
vaguely familiar—reacquaint ourselves
with mud and rain, with one another.

SEPTEMBER DAWN

But God himself comes often and stays long,
when the castrati's singing disturbs Him.
- Ranier Maria Rilke ("The Voices")

Within the quietude of dawn
streaked in yellow flame
between charred black shadows

when the sun peeks low beneath
the branches shedding leaves,
I hear voices in the canyon,

from the ridges and the draws,
of the generations gathered
where women left their track

ground in stone, and men
built barns and fences,
some yet leaning into time

unknown, for a different breed
of cattle and of dreams—
a chorus clear and strong.

And all the working hands
that left no mark upon the land
they still inhabit singing

harmony and peace
within the quietude of dawn
streaked in yellow flame.

BLASPHEMIES

We may blame the invisible
deities, the almighty powers
we can't see work

against us—toying with
what makes us tick
to urgent clocks.

And we may find relief
damning them
with metaphors, similes

and alliterative profanity
as if the gods were deaf
to rehearsed poetry.

But best to save energy
turning blasphemies loose
just under our breaths.

ANOTHER RELIGION

It could be spring in November
waiting for a rain, yet we worry
about weather we can't control—

complain to gods we have invented:
separate specialists leaving signs
we let tease and disappoint us

within the space we vest our lives.
But the Glory Hallelujah chorus
roars when it storms off every hillside,

pours down draws. Yet beneath dark sky
duels of thunderbolts, heavens at war,
we cherish our electric helplessness

and raise a glass to Gods all.
It could be spring in November, or
another religion for which we ride.

WIND UNDER MY SKIN

…not likely wanting to be anywhere
or anyone else.
– Jim Harrison ("Burning the Ditches")

ON THE SEMI-ARID EDGE

The big dogs are drilling deeper,
pumping the last of a million years
of underground water, each river

dammed into furrows to farm
the empty *Laguna de Tache.*
Sixty years ago, when red lights

stopped in every railroad town,
colorful cornucopias spilled
from billboards onto Highway 99

bragging fruit or vegetable capitals
of another world, and huge Big Oranges
squeezed juice every ten miles.

On the semi-arid edge of change,
we pray for rain and dream of floods
to take this Valley back in time.

OCTOBER, 2015

Those that survive will talk
about the 'Drought of Two-Thirteen'
after damn-little rain in 2012
before the summer:

>   day after day,
>   100 degrees
>   or more we endured,
>   trancelike—

an incarceration, our waterfed
submission of the flesh flushed,
we sweat like beasts—let
the unimportant run down our hocks.

October now is brown,
dust dulls autumn leaves
and dirt shows all the way to the top
of every hill and mountain.

Not just the ground around
shrinking waterholes pounded fine
by pad and hoof,
but the whole nine yards

of foothills from Fresno
to Bakersfield—we are
smack-dab in the middle
of our own damn Dust Bowl.

WIND UNDER MY SKIN

I stumble on Bukowski early in the dark
morning, pleased to hear him voice
basic town stuff from the other side

of the page, but glad he's not been
riding shotgun through this drought,
cussing everyone including God.

We hung a little hope on the gray
rolling in, gathering on the ridges—
on gusts stirring up, then down canyon

and grinned like foolish children
who still believed in weathermen
and Santa Claus. We dreamed

of how much rain it would take
to fill all the new cracks in clay
where the thin grass fades—

of an errant thunderstorm
that could fill the dirt tanks
and let the creek run

enough to meander and pool
under canopies of sycamores and oaks
for the Wood Ducks, cattle and us.

Through the black screen door,
wind under my skin,
I hear it begin to rain.

RAISONS D'ÊTRE

Now in the quiet I stand
and look at her a long time, glad
to have recovered what is lost
in the exchange of something for money.
- Wendell Berry ("The Sorrel Filly")

Looming closer, a swirling darkness just beyond
the thought of summer's water that is not
frozen deep in the Sierras to feed our rivers

and canyon leaks—of brittle fall and cattle
gathered at an empty trough. The creek dries back
and sinks in March, lifted to new canopies

of sycamores dressing. Skeletons of old oaks
stand out between greening survivors, some
wearing only clumps of yellow mistletoe

hanging like reasons, *raisons*—like raisins
clinging to a leafless vine. Each season
spins the same dry song, yet we find our place,

harmonize and sing along, lifted like precious
moisture to tender leaves, a basic evasion not
available in the big box stores, unrecorded

in the history of our presence. This may be
the new normal for old people—that daze
of amazement we have been working towards.

THESE YEARS OF DROUGHT

No frost, morning warm—
flotilla of round clouds,
a raft of ships scouting

for a dark fleet, big guns
on the horizon. A welcome
invasion of the flesh:

earth, roots, bark, blade
and mind's eye open—yet
now afraid of a real rain,

to be drunk with it—
to let go and be ravaged
at last, to turn loose the dry

and dusty lines of poetry,
my plodding momentum tied
to bare dirt and empty skies—

afraid to howl, to learn
the language of the gods,
to speak in tongues

and dance with trees
far from my secure delirium,
these years of drought.

ELKO SNOW

On the wind beyond the window,
snowflakes sideways, the street
streams with white waves, riffles

on gusts colliding with vehicles
to swirl like dust on a black
river of asphalt. I am no snow man

and imagine small coveys of quail
before the shotgun, before
the bobcat, before taking flight.

Feathers fly with each collision,
gather and flee downstream
as if running for their lives.

WINTER MOLECULES

Solids, liquids, and gases move.
This could be Oregon
moisture falling into drought—
the hard and dry begins to slip
and slide with the magnetic pull
of each, releasing me to supposing
why I'm drawn to certain people,
places, mountains, trees and rocks
come alive—ions spinning webs to hold
my eye, my flesh, my open mind.

DAMP WIND

When the wind blows up canyon,
first light gray,
I am the old red horse,
twenty-five, bucking in place.

We never loose it, that wanting
stirred and satisfied—
to be wild again
when everything is right.

We feel his feeble effort,
hooves barely off the ground,
our whoops and cheers
howling on a damp wind.

EL NIÑO FOREPLAY

Long on promises, she moves closer,
a slow seductive dance lightly touching,
barely brushing the roof before she leaves

in the dark. I am too old to chase
blindly, and wait instead for words
to fall upon the page when she returns—

or not. I believe she means business.
How she loves to tease the be-Jesus
right out of me. It makes her feel good

to see me uncomfortable, vulnerable
to her every gesture, the stormy look
of these hills wrapped in gray gossamer

dawn waits to unfold at first light
if I'm lucky—if I'm patient enough
to let her have her way with me.

IDES OF SEPTEMBER

It is nothing, really, but a damp breeze
through the screen door rattling papers
on my desk, clearing the evidence

of last night's flat bread from the kitchen
before returning to morning black—
light drops on a metal roof.

Fourth dry summer of drought,
it sweeps dust from my brain,
teases hair on my bare chest

as if I were wild, alive again—
as if we might escape this hell,
rinse the taste from our mouths.

Too early to storm, it is nothing, really,
but a damp breeze playing rain—
a few gods revisiting survivors

and the dead—playing with the possibility
of change. Once again, I am reminded
that nothing stays the same.

ENOUGH

Sing me a dry song, something
somewhere else you learned to chant
under your breath. Mesmerizing,

they stand half-dressed in morning light
in a pool of golden leaves, Solstice
peeking low under the door, showing just

enough bark that I forget the words to this
chorus of sycamores, my dancing winter
nymphs trying-on new outfits—posing,

having fun showing me what I have not seen.
Sing me your dry song, share the mantra
of the plodding before they prove:

a drought can be beautiful and soothing.
But better yet, bring me a hard rain, so
we can get naked and start over again.

KEEPING SECRETS

How do they know, these old fat cows
that read a baggy sadness in my walk
among them checking irons as they pull

alfalfa stems apart to tongue green leaf
in the corral? The gates are set, waiting
for the truck to town. There is nothing

right about the moment, this they know—
little consolation in my voice, they eye me
suspiciously searching for details

in my muted gestures. If I told them
all I know of town, of auction rings
and rails, they would try to escape

to brushy hills, lay fences down
to take their chances without water
through the summer—this I know.

READING CATTLE

The weeks take wing and flutter
like coveys of quail to safety,
seasons spin into one another

as the dawn rides up and down,
north and south, upon the ridgeline,
never resting in the same place twice

no matter the year—this moment
unique. And these old eyes
still sharp at a distance, see more

than they used to—know the details
to look for. I am learning how
to talk with my eyes, conversations

accompanied with gentle words:
reverberating murmurs within
my chest, from land we understand.

GOLDEN RULE

I would like to say that thinking
like cattle is preferable to humans
who need immediate answers

and science to prove them right,
whose urgency demands action
and reaction until the herd's

thundering hooves stampede
the earth into atomic dust.
Cattle would not press any matter

enough to destroy themselves,
but rather play domestic than wild
given time to weigh your wishes.

Making sense of them you must
be cordial, shed your fear and anger—
try to remember the Golden Rule.

BORN IN A DROUGHT

Islands of bare, red clay
on shallow green receding—
seeds that never swelled

to root ceramic slopes
or left with clouds
from cloven hooves—

stare back sternly.
She is dry,
nothing left to offer

the eye.
The lone calf
grazing shores

for the overlooked
knows no better
world than this.

INTO WINTER

Slowly the sun creeps across the floor;
it is coming your way. It touches your shoe.
- William Stafford ("It's All Right")

All the shades of brown are crisp now,
mid-December light, shadows linger
to look like cows frozen on bare hillsides,

leaves litter the dry creek bed as sycamores
show flesh, willows burn in between
like lanterns. Blue Oaks become frightened

skeletons on the run. It is a drought
and it is beautiful, everything giving-up
at once, looking to die. The top heavy

flatbed stacked another layer high
squats and groans down the road,
string of thin black cows following

inside the barbed wire like perfectly
disciplined children—all makes sense.
It's simple now for quite awhile.

USDA CHOICE

Loose upon this earth
we mark our presence
like dogs at dusk,

blaze trees
and build fence
to claim our place

in time, to sleep
at peace
with the outside world

of Phillistines gone wild.
We fill their bowls
with beef.

WET SPRING

The trails are gone,
hats above a sea of wild oats
like navigating ground fog

blind to rocks and ruts
in a slow gather
bringing tunnels together,

cows and calves. All the brags
of tying knots above the withers,
dally wraps around the horn,

ring tame and distant—
even the best broke horse
can't resist temptation.

NEAR AUSTIN, NEVADA

Left 100 miles
towards Tonopah, dry hay
for California.

HARBINGER

The scouts arrive to paint
blue denim skies with fuzzy
promises of rain.

RAIN GAUGE

Not much to measure
but cobwebs and leaves in June—
ready nonetheless.

AFTER RAIN

Sun sets on the sighs
that cling to wet hills breathing
color into clouds.

AFTER RAIN 2

Dawn's soft light steaming
rain's last embrace still clinging,
love spent overnight.

REMNANTS OF BLANCA

Like furious gods,
magnificent thunderheads
rising above us.

DARK LIGHT

Errant gods return
to paint earth and sky, bring
dark light after dry.

PETRICHOR

Into thirsty flesh
we inhale the smell of rain
upon dry grasses.

HANGOVER

Slow to leave after
a night rain, the clouds still want
to party at dawn.

AFTER THANKSGIVING

I stumble out of an old dream panicked
about cattle I haven't checked in months
on a hidden ranch I can't place, connect
except they were not grazing vineyard rows
with no fences, not loose in town this time,
but on some hard-to-gather rolling ground
you can't see from the pocked asphalt road
snaking through blond summer foothills.

Last time, they were OK, bull calves
too big to brand breeding sisters, but alive
on good feed and water. It may have been
the turkey dressing drenched in juices,
or the cranberries fermenting fear familiar
that I recognize more than this imagined place
to wait before saddling a horse, loading up
asleep to tilt at impossible windmills.

I've been here before, rusty wire on redwood
posts askew, exploring canyons, finding old
rough-haired families too weak to be wild—
all the guilt and disappointment I need
to torture my subconscious. Too old for that,
I roll over to let my weak knees hang before
testing with a first step towards reality:
cigarette, coffee and a poem for Black Friday.

THE SONG

It's not about you—
and not about to change
the weather or politics.

You are helpless,
at the mercy of the swirl
of elements colliding,

ricochets and explosions,
occasional clear views
of space and landscape

that keep you leaning forward
into the sun, your shadow cast
upon a fading track of small

accomplishment. After a rain
every tree frog sings
as if spring depended on it.

BLACK SKIES

Dark morning without moon or stars
before the first winter storm, the day before
Black Friday rains deals and discounts

for Christmas, for our economy and I am
ever thankful that the bulls are out early
courting cows, meeting kids and family

before dirt roads get too slick to travel—
ever thankful for the drought that felled
two big Live Oaks on the gate and fence

we corded-up and stacked beneath the eave
before the girls drove posts and spliced
the barbed wire on a mat of green

to leave disorder looking like a park—ever
thankful for them, for you and this ground
we're invested in together, for good horses

willing to get the cow work done—
black skies without moon or stars,
you and I alone before the storm.

FIRST WINTER STORM, 2016

Wind bangs against the mountains,
cold on warm rips and tears
cracks in air as crooked fingers
touch the ground with 'lectric
yellow light to spark a roar
upon the metal roof in panting
pulses beneath soft gray
as if the gods were making love
in a bass drum, small canyon room
upstairs spawning muddy rivulets
towards a dry creek bed between
wet sycamores undressing
long white limbs suggestively
spilling November tans and browns
upon the green to stand naked
before an eager flow gathering
rafts of clothes upstream—

or as angry as the 60s
marching to make love
instead of war, or vice versa—

or with the best intentions
for all we've done today,
come to wash the dirty laundry,
our tracks and waste away.

PEGASUS

Sometimes we ride high enough
to see the backs of eagles, bronze
wings tracing steep hillside oats

a glide. Even horses pause
to take notice. You can feel envy
rise beneath you, becoming one

another for a moment—prolonged
instants we crave, yet cannot hold
with minds a grip. But letting go

we float the thermals to Olympus
to bring back lightning, thunder—
and with luck a poem and some rain.

BLACK INK

Crown on ice
waiting for a rain
in a water glass

for me and this
yellow pad
to storm black ink,

prolong spring
with fresh metaphors
for resilience.

TOGETHER

And note this, dear dead doctor:
When we sleep, our legs twitch,
And not from the hunt
But from trying to run away.
- Gary Soto ("Dr. Freud, Please")

A Red Tail pair in Blue Oak tops, buff breasts bared
to glow at first light, watch over their dark shoulders
as I feed hay, speak to horses, winter mornings

to wonder about the everyday routines that tie us
to animals, to a place and time by the sun. The deer
would lay down where the barn stands now

over a shrinking stack of bales, a short walk
to metal mangers as I look back through the eyes
of the house to see you moving to the woodstove,

curls of Manzanita smoke disappear into the gray.
We have camped in the trail between canyons of wild
pad and hoof, claimed the space they walk around

and would take back should we be gone for long
without our habits holding what we've done together,
together—for this moment we hold our ground.

for Robbin

ACKNOWLEDGEMENTS

For the kind support of Gary Snyder whose hands-on example gave me the courage to write poetry fifty years ago; for Wendell Berry's sense of place; for William Stafford's discipline and line of thought; for Jim Harrison's leaps; and for Robinson Jeffers, a solid rock. For my family at the Western Folklife Center who have offered a venue and purpose for my notion of poetry; for recognition and validation from the National Cowboy and Western Heritage Museum and the Academy of Western Artists. For the encouragement from Red Shuttleworth and Bunchgrass Press for publishing a number of these poems in his chapbook anthologies "You Should Know" and "Ask Yourself". For Sylvia Ross, my literary confidant. For her support and many tweets circulating my poems and photography, Margo Metegrano, Director of the Center for Western and Cowboy Poetry.

For our many friends and neighbors here at home, out-of-state and out-of-country, we are inspired and blessed. Most of all for Robbin's love and partnership without which these poems would not read the same, or be written at all. Whether assessing our cows, grass or water resources, we have shared the same eyes despite our individual perspectives, for our evenings discussing cattle and the ranch, noting new observations and penning our deck poems in the open air that so often bleed into the early-morning writing of this collection.